Take time on a walk to stop and pet a dog.
The act of touching an animal
releases oxytocin, the same feel-good,
calming hormone released during orgasm
and breastfeeding—two things that are
much harder to accomplish on the street.

Indulge yourself. A few brownies never made anyone fat, so allow yourself the occasional treat and enjoy every moment of it.
Better yet, make them yourself:

- *Preheat the oven to 350 degrees.*
- *In a saucepan over low heat, melt 8 Tbsp. butter cut into pieces; turn off the heat and add 6 oz. chopped semisweet or bittersweet chocolate pieces and whisk until smooth. Let sit for 10 minutes; whisk in ¾ cup sugar, two eggs, and 1 tsp. vanilla; add ½ cup flour and a dash of salt. Put the batter in a buttered 8-inch square pan and bake about 25 minutes.*

"The most effective way to do it

is to do it."

~ AMELIA EARHART

We know that laughter acts as an antidepressant,
but new research shows it to be as powerful
as meditation when it comes to de-stressing
the brain. To give yourself a double whammy of
calming bliss, try a laughing meditation. Start by
sitting quietly and turning up the corners of
your mouth into a smile. Even if your first response
is the nervous giggles, you're already halfway there.

As much as you can, don't waste energy

comparing yourself to other people. There are

no magic tricks beyond taking care of yourself

the best you can, and no one has her act perfectly

together—she probably just has better

under-eye concealer. Ask her what it is!

Start every morning with beautiful words

by subscribing to a daily poem online.

It's food for the mind and the soul.

"And so taking the long way home through the market I slow my pace down. It doesn't come naturally. My legs are programmed to trot briskly and my arms to pump up and down like pistons, but I force myself to stroll past the stalls and pavement cafés. To enjoy just **being** *somewhere, rather than rushing from somewhere, to somewhere. Inhaling deep lungfuls of air, instead of my usual shallow breaths. I take a moment to just stop and look around me. And smile to myself.*

For the first time in a long time, I can, quite literally, smell the coffee."

~ Alexandra Potter
The Two Lives of Miss Charlotte Merryweather

*"Women need real moments
of solitude and self-reflection
to balance out how much
of ourselves we give away."*

~ Barbara De Angelis

Whatever happens, know you can handle it.

Choose to confront situations with grace

and they become more manageable.

Once they're resolved, let them

become part of the past.

Make your bathroom a respite of calm
with these cabinet essentials:
lavender bubble bath, essential rose oil
to drop into the water, lotion,
and several scented candles.

"Always go with the choice that scares you the most—because that's the one that is going to require the most from you."

~ CAROLINE MYSS

Pick one painting at a museum

that you love or have always wanted to see.

Walk straight to it without looking at

anything else. Sit in front of the painting

for a full 20 minutes so you can really

appreciate it. It will stay with you for days.

Book a monthly date night with yourself.

Go to a movie or out for dinner at a restaurant

you've been dying to try.

There are some things worth paying extra for,

like already-cleaned shrimp, precut carrots,

and the perfect pair of jeans.

"Cherish your solitude

Take trains by yourself to places you have never been

Sleep out alone under the stars

Learn how to drive a stick shift

Go so far away that you stop being afraid

of not coming back

Say no when you don't want to do something

Say yes if your instincts are strong,

even if everyone around you disagrees

Decide whether you want to be liked or admired

Decide if fitting in is more important than finding

out what you're doing here.

Believe in kissing

Fight for tenderness

Care as much as you do"

~ EVE ENSLER
I Am an Emotional Creature

Create inner calm by not procrastinating.

Instead of spending time dreading

something you need to do, just do it.

You wipe it off your list and get

to be proud of yourself as well.

Turn your life upside down! Delight in one headstand every day (the wall is an excellent spotter if you need a little extra balance—and in general, who doesn't?). Yoga enthusiasts believe that inversions are good for flushing toxins from the body and even increasing sex drive. No scientific study is needed to know that practicing literal balance and a change of perspective is the antidote to a busy day.

A facial will make you look rested and rosy. No need to take the time at or spend the money for a spa—you can pamper yourself at home while you kick back and watch your favorite TV show:

- *Mash up a medium banana into a paste.*
- *Add ¼ cup plain yogurt and 2 Tbsp. honey; you can also add in a few drops of lavender oil.*
- *Apply in a thin layer and leave on for 20 minutes.*

Buy one pair of pants and a dress that always make you feel like you're the perfect weight. Feeling good about your body is nothing short of a miracle cure for stress.

Ask yourself what would make you happy. Too often we ruminate on the things that are making us feel bad and forget what it is we actually want. Make a list. Then put stars next to the items you have the power to make happen for yourself. Put reminders in places you will see them.

Keep a beautiful flower

in a bud vase on your desk.

When you look at it, remind yourself

of all the beauty in the world and

how lucky you are to be a part of it.

"You grow up the day you have your

first real laugh—at yourself."

~ ETHEL BARRYMORE

When you feel overwhelmed, repeat this
to yourself until you remember that it's true:
You'll get it all done. You always have.

Take five minutes to unsubscribe from companies
whose regular emails you end up deleting daily.
An uncluttered inbox is the new uncluttered closet.

"Sometimes I have loved the peacefulness of an ordinary Sunday. It is like standing in a newly planted garden after a warm rain. You can feel the silent and invisible life."

~ MARILYNNE ROBINSON

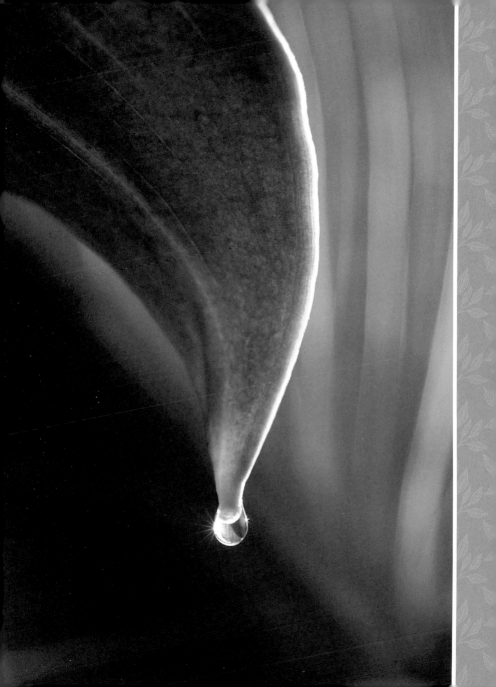

You'll never stress about getting dressed
as long as your closet has:

- *Instantly comforting flannel pajamas—and elegant silk ones*
- *An oversize, overly worn shirt and boxer shorts—and also a lace nightgown*
- *Boyfriend jeans just big enough to make you feel slim and skinny jeans just tight enough to make you feel sexy*
- *A beat-up pair of motorcycle boots and a pair of stiletto boots to pair with your moods*
- *A black cashmere twinset and a faded, cozy sweatshirt*
- *A tailored black blazer and a funky leather jacket*
- *A fitted white button-down and a slouchy white tee*
- *. . . And of course a little black dress or three*

Remember that you can only do *your* part

in any situation. Do the best you can.

That is more than enough.

"Understand that the right to choose your own path is a sacred privilege. Use it. Dwell in possibility."

~ OPRAH WINFREY

"Everything changes. The leaves, the weather,
the color of your hair, the texture of your skin.
The feelings you have today—whether they kill you
or enthrall you—won't be the same tomorrow,
so let go. Celebrate. Enjoy. Nothing lasts, except
your decision to celebrate everything, everyone,
for the beauty that is there within each moment,
each smile, each impermanent flicker of infinity."

~ VIRONIKA TUGALEVA

Once a week, turn off your phone

and computer at 8 p.m.

Get into bed with a book

and stay there until lights out.

Change your email password so it inspires you or reminds you of your intentions to find a few minutes of peace a day. Try out combinations like these:

- *Bed@Before12*
- *KeepCalm&CarryOn*
- *UCanDoThi$*
- *1Day@ATime*
- *WatchYrEgo*
- *TakeAbre@th*
- *ItJutChattr*

Keep a small, pretty memo pad and a pen you love in your purse at all times. When something starts to nag at you—even if it's just an errand you need to run—write it down and then let it go.

"A woman is like a tea bag—

you never know how strong she is

until she gets in hot water."

~ AMERICAN PROVERB

"We need to accept that we won't always make the right decisions, that we'll screw up royally sometimes—understanding that failure is not the opposite of success, it's part of success."

~ ARIANNA HUFFINGTON

If you're not going to be worried about something in five years, it's not worth worrying about now. Consider the weight of the worry (next week, will you even remember the traffic jam you're sitting in?) and then mentally put it in its rightful box, marked "irrelevant."

Our feet and ankles contain a quarter
of the bones in our bodies, as well as
100 muscles, ligaments, and tendons.
We thank them for all their hard work
by stuffing them into high heels.
Make amends and book
a reflexology appointment!

Brew yourself a cup of calming herbal tea before going to bed; make enough to put the remainder in the refrigerator for a quick, refreshing iced version the next day.

When you walk in the door at the end of the day,

put down your bag and take off your shoes as

a signal to yourself that you're *done*. And try not

to fetch your phone back out of your purse

for at least half an hour.

Switch your focus from stressful challenges
to positive ones. Go to a yoga class,
climb a wall, finally learn to swim the crawl . . .
anything that you've never tried before.
In addition to taking your mind off
daily distractions, tackling something
new can help you learn to see obstacles
as positive—especially when they result
in six-pack abs!

Keep your pantry stocked with easy-to-store basics and you can cook yourself this hearty homemade dinner in minutes flat:

- *Cook pasta according to package instructions.*
- *While the pasta cooks, sauté garlic in olive oil, add in a couple of anchovies until they dissolve, stir in red pepper flakes, and add a 15 oz. can of tomato sauce. If you want to turn it into a puttanesca sauce, simply add capers and black olives. Toss with cooked pasta.*
- *Sprinkle with a little Parmesan cheese, pour a glass of wine, and toast yourself!*

Consider investing in a white noise machine. A Yale University study found that noise stress—which we experience thanks to sirens, horns, and noisy neighbors—impaired cognitive function in monkeys' brains. As if we needed any proof the morning after a bad night's sleep!

Carve out time in your schedule to volunteer.

Studies have shown that giving to others

increases happiness and lowers stress levels.

It's good for the body and soul!

"If you remain calm in the midst of great chaos, it is the surest guarantee that it will eventually subside."

~ JULIE ANDREWS EDWARDS
The Last of the Really Great Whangdoodles

Set your alarm for 15 minutes earlier than usual.
Savor your coffee, read the paper from front
to back, and enjoy a morning of moving slowly.

Download a guided meditation.

Instead of texting, emailing,

or talking on the phone, listen to that

on your way to work.

Learn to ask for help, especially for small things.

Reach out to another parent to take your child

to school when you need a day to linger a few extra

minutes at home; ask a coworker to look over

a project before you hand it in to catch any errors—

real or imagined—that might keep you up at night.

Friends are eager to do something nice for us,

but they can't read our minds.

"Forgiveness is not always easy.

At times, it feels more painful than

the wound we suffered, to forgive

the one that inflicted it. And yet,

there is no peace without forgiveness."

~ MARIANNE WILLIAMSON
Illuminata

"Gorgeous, amazing things come into our lives when we are paying attention: mangoes, grandnieces, Bach, ponds. This happens more often when we have as little expectation as possible ... Astonishing material and revelation appear in our lives all the time. Let it be. Unto us, so much is given. We just have to be open for business."

~ ANNE LAMOTT
Help, Thanks, Wow: The Three Essential Prayers

Make tonight the night

you get enough sleep.

SPECIAL EXCUSE

———

Date..............................

.....................................(Name) is excused

Going from ....to.....................

Time leaving ....
                                              Signature

Returning from ....to.....................

Time leaving ....
                                              Signature

Write yourself a hall pass for something

you don't want to do and don't *really* have to,

like a cocktail party or an unnecessary work

or school event.

"Because while you are imagining,

you might as well imagine

something worth while."

~ L. M. MONTGOMERY
Anne of Green Gables

Whine it out. Admitting to a friend
that you sometimes hate being a mother
and occasionally wish your partner would go
be someone else's will not only make you
feel better (and maybe even laugh)—it'll also
give her permission to do the same.

It's not possible to do more than one thing at once (at least not well). Accept that you will not be the first human to change this. Practice paying attention only to the task at hand. Guide yourself back with the one-word reminder so powerful it even works on dogs and children: "Focus!"

"Dedicate yourself to the good

you deserve and desire for yourself.

Give yourself peace of mind.

You deserve to be happy.

You deserve delight."

~ HANNAH ARENDT

*"You may not always have
a comfortable life. And you will not
always be able to solve all the world's
problems all at once. But don't ever
underestimate the impact you can have,
because history has shown us that
courage can be contagious, and hope
can take on a life of its own."*

~ MICHELLE OBAMA

Turn your back to your computer when
you're on the phone so you can
really listen to what's being said.
Even better: Leave the room.

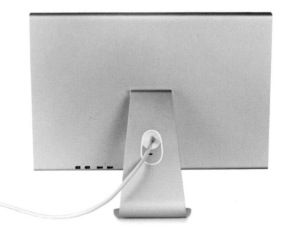

Replace the lightbulb in the lamp by your bed
with a pink-tinted one. The switch will create
a calming, soft glow.

"Have regular hours for work and play,

make each day both useful and pleasant,

and prove that you understand the worth of time

by employing it well. Then youth will be delightful,

old age will bring few regrets, and life

become a beautiful success."

~ LOUISA MAY ALCOTT
Little Women

"No matter who you are,

no matter what you did,

no matter where you've come from,

you can always change,

become a better version of yourself."

~ MADONNA

Relax your standards and begin with
the premise that everyone is doing his
or her best. It's a waste of energy to find fault
in people for not living up to your ideals;
instead, practice celebrating all that
the people around you *do* accomplish!

"Some prefer the wildness . . .
Some the calm. There's enough
of both in the world for everyone to
have their choice. And enough time
for any to change their mind."

~ NORA ROBERTS
Born in Shame

If things aren't going easily in your life,

that doesn't necessarily mean they're going badly.

Trying situations are often the times we learn

the most lasting lessons—especially about

how to comfort and calm ourselves.

Ease your own burdens as well as a friend's.
Ask a neat friend to help you clean out your closets
in exchange for making her dinner. If another
is tech-savvy, offer to babysit her kids
while she installs useful apps on your phone.
Remember: You're not in this alone.

*"We cannot change
what we are unaware of,
and once we are aware,
we cannot help but change."*

~ SHERYL SANDBERG
*Lean In: Women, Work,
and the Will to Lead*

Treat your bookshelf like a beloved library—
a beautiful place you stop and linger.
Fill the shelves with a few must-haves:

- *A tantalizing mystery* (From Doon With Death, *by Ruth Rendell*)
- *A tried-and-true classic you can pick up again and again* (Pride and Prejudice, *by Jane Austen*)
- *A great—and dark—romance novel* (Jane Eyre, *by Charlotte Brontë*)
- *A Pulitzer Prize winner* (The Poisonwood Bible, *by Barbara Kingsolver*)
- *A book of essays to make you laugh* (I Feel Bad About My Neck, *by Nora Ephron*)
- *A book that makes you believe in magic* (The House of the Spirits, *by Isabel Allende*)
- *Inspiring poetry* (The Complete Poetry, *by Maya Angelou*)
- *A powerful memoir* (H is for Hawk, *by Helen Macdonald*)

"We need time to defuse, to contemplate. Just as in sleep our brains relax and give us dreams, so at some time in the day we need to disconnect, reconnect, and look around us."

~ LAURIE COLWIN

We all have people we love who spend
their time complaining, invariably making us
feel worse and them no better. Instead of
sitting through a meal of it, ask them to join you
for a brisk walk, an exercise class, or a movie
so you can do something relaxing—and good!—
for yourself while they unload.

Think about one thing that will make your life

easier tomorrow and vow to do it. It can be

as simple as packing your gym bag the night before

or buying that one extra phone charger

to leave in another room.

"I am thankful the most important key in history was invented. It's not the key to your house, your car, your boat, your safety deposit box, your bike lock, or your private community. It's the key to order, sanity, and peace of mind. The key is 'Delete.'"

~ ELAYNE BOOSLER

"You may encounter many defeats,

but you must not be defeated.

In fact, the encountering may

be the very experience which creates

the vitality and the power to endure."

~ Maya Angelou

Throw out your scale.
Attaching a feeling of self-worth to
an ever fluctuating number, let alone
first thing in the morning, is insanity.
Your jeans will tell you all you need
to know on the subject.

When you look at your calendar on Sunday night,

make sure there is one thing in the upcoming

week that you are looking forward to. If not,

add one ASAP! Anticipatory anxiety is terrible;

anticipatory happiness is joy.

"In the midst of happiness or despair

in sorrow or in joy

in pleasure or in pain:

Do what is right and you will be at peace."

~ JESS ROTHENBERG
The Catastrophic History of You and Me

Instead of making excuses,

make a policy of being (kindly) honest.

It's liberating to say, "I'm sorry—

I just have too much going on

right now to plan one more thing!"

And it's liberating for your friends,

who might follow your example.

We all make unhealthy choices.

Finished off the chocolate chip cookies?

Had an extra glass of wine (or two)? Join the club.

Now double your pleasure by skipping over

the regret. There's no need to beat yourself up.

You can atone tomorrow—or better yet,

forget about it!

There are few experiences more stressful
than an argument with someone you love.
Going forward, try to apologize as quickly
as you can so you can both move on instead
of stewing. It's a surefire way to inject serenity
into your relationships.

"To sit with a dog on a hillside on a glorious afternoon is to be back in Eden, where doing nothing was not boring—it was peace."

~ MILAN KUNDERA

*"In spite of everything I see all around me
every day, in spite of all the times I cry when
I read the newspaper, I have a shaky assurance
that everything will turn out fine. I don't think
I'm the only one. Why else would the phrase
'Everything's all right' ease a deep and troubled
place in so many of us? We just don't know,
we never know so much, yet we have such faith.
We hold our hands over our hurts
and lean forward, full of yearning and forgiveness.
It is how we keep on, this kind of hope."*

~ ELIZABETH BERG
Talk Before Sleep

Schedule 45 minutes to exercise three times
a week. Treat it as you would a meeting
with your boss: non-negotiable.
Showing up is often the entire battle ...
... And when you really can't bear
the idea of exercising for those 45 minutes,
tell yourself you only need to do seven.
Studies show that if you can make it that far,
you're generally in for the rest!

To feel confident in the world, know how to:

- *Change a tire*
- *Write a thank-you note*
- *Order a bottle of wine*
- *Tip properly and without embarrassment*
- *Roast a chicken*
- *Make a budget and stick to it*
- *Keep your passport current (you never know!)*
- *Be your own best date*

"I will be calm.

I will be mistress of myself."

~ JANE AUSTEN
Sense and Sensibility

Start a gift drawer or closet. Pick up
extra candles, copies of books you love,
beautiful scarves that you think would
make for great gifts for your friends and family
(even better if you can think ahead during sales!).
Cutting back on last-minute shopping
puts hours back into your life.

"No person, no place, and no thing
has any power over us, for 'we' are
the only thinkers in our mind.
When we create peace and harmony
and balance in our minds,
we will find it in our lives."

~ LOUISE L. HAY
You Can Heal Your Life

Don't sit on resentment for another second. If a friend has let you down, find a way to let them know; they may be blissfully unaware while you're grinding your teeth. Ask the person in question out for a drink to hit the reset button in your own mind. By reminding yourself why they matter in the first place, you'll address and resolve any lingering upset.

"You cannot find peace

by avoiding life."

~ MICHAEL CUNNINGHAM
The Hours

Try not to attach emotions to your emotions.

There's nothing wrong with being angry or sad;

judging how you feel—on top of feeling it—

keeps you stuck in the negative longer.

Take a day-trip adventure: Hop on a train or bus
to somewhere close to home you've never
been before. You don't need to invest a lot of time
or money to have a vacation from your daily life!

Remember the childhood joys of dressing up? Capture that feeling again by exchanging your studs for fun, dangling earrings and your everyday necklace for a funky bib-like collar. Keep a "happy" jewelry box where you store accessories to turn your mood around with the click of a clasp.

"Time you enjoy wasting

is not wasted time."

~ MARTHE TROLY-CURTIN
Phrynette Married

Take a ten-minute nap. Studies show that

a little midday snooze as short as that makes us

sharper and more serene. If you think

your life is too frantic to steal ten minutes

of shut-eye, better make it twenty.

Your mother was right: Often the doctor knows best. An annual physical can turn up common vitamin deficiencies you aren't aware you have that are causing symptoms like fatigue. A few weeks of the appropriate supplements and you may feel like your most rested and relaxed self.

"Wherever there's laughter,

there is heaven."

~ MADELEINE L'ENGLE
A Ring of Endless Light

Email has made the world an increasingly generic and impersonal place. When you need to have an intimate and important conversation, pick up the phone instead of turning to your keyboard. You'll avoid misunderstandings that can arise from one-sided missives.

"Be thankful for what you have;
you'll end up having more.
If you concentrate on
what you don't have,
you will never,
ever have enough."

~ OPRAH WINFREY

When you're feeling stressed out,

drop your tongue to the bottom of your mouth.

This will automatically unclench your jaw;

the rest of your body will follow.

"Silence more musical

than any song."

~ CHRISTINA ROSSETTI

Do something that scares you—in the kitchen. Pick a favorite dish you've always thought impossible to make at home. Luxuriate in taking the time to understand what goes into it. When you feel you've mastered it, invite a friend or two over to share in your accomplishment. Every opportunity to build your confidence in small ways makes you more confident in the world.

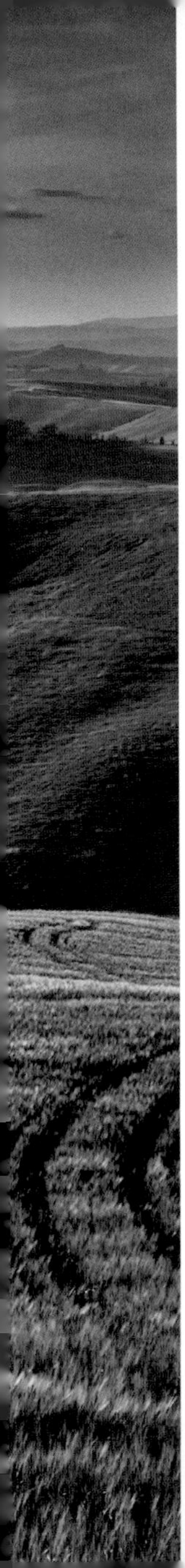

"We don't realize that,

somewhere within us all,

there does exist a supreme Self

who is eternally at peace."

~ ELIZABETH GILBERT
Eat, Pray, Love

The next time you catch yourself feeling

anxious about something that *may* happen,

remind yourself that worries are only ghost stories

we tell ourselves about the future.

You are not responsible for other adults'

emotional lives. Be as kind as you can be

and apologize when you are not.

But remember that you are not going to fix

other people's broken pieces.

"Your life is an occasion.

Rise to it."

~ SUZANNE WEYN
Mr. Magorium's Wonder Emporium

Don't let email be the first thing you read
in the morning. Instead, begin the day in a way
that doesn't demand interaction (or a possible
reaction!). Page through a hard copy of the
newspaper over coffee or keep a book of poetry
by your bed and read one beautiful poem
before you get up.

Make a list of your positive qualities—
both things you like about yourself
and things others like about you.
Read it occasionally before bed
or when you are brushing your teeth
in the morning, until you know it by heart.
The next time you're feeling down
on yourself, reflect on these attributes
that are yours alone.

On a day you're feeling very happy, go and buy
a perfume you love. Every time you wear it,
bring yourself back to the way you felt that day.

It's impossible to balance it all—work, kids, friends, getting dinner on the table—and never feel stressed. Have a phrase at the ready that comforts you. The next time you're feeling yourself fretting over something you can't change, quickly replace it with one of these mantras:

- *"Get through today. I'll do better tomorrow."*
- *"I'm doing the best I can."*
- *"This is going to pass, and when it does, I will do something nice for myself."*
- *"One step at a time; it will all get done."*

*"We should learn to accept
that change is truly the only thing
that's going on always, and learn
to ride with it and enjoy it."*

~ ALICE WALKER

"After all those years as a woman hearing
'not thin enough, not pretty enough,
not smart enough, not this enough,
not that enough,' almost overnight
I woke up one morning and thought,
'I'm enough.'"

~ ANNA QUINDLEN

Say something nice to a stranger.

"Well, now I know I can control my tongue,

my temper, and my appetites, but that's it.

I have no effect on weather, traffic, or luck.

I can't make good things happen. I can't keep

anybody safe. I can't influence the future

and I can't fix up the past.

What a relief."

~ ABIGAIL THOMAS
A Three Dog Life

"The most beautiful people we have known
are those who have known defeat,
known suffering, known struggle,
known loss, and have found their way out
of the depths. These persons have
an appreciation, a sensitivity,
and an understanding of life that
fills them with compassion, gentleness,
and a deep loving concern.
Beautiful people do not just happen."

~ ELISABETH KÜBLER-ROSS
Death: The Final Stage of Growth

At bedtime, make yourself a soothing,
warm vanilla milk: It has all the comfort
of hot chocolate without the caffeine.

- *In a saucepan, combine 1 cup of milk with 1 to 2 Tbsp. of sugar, depending on your taste; once the sugar has dissolved, stir in ½ tsp. of vanilla.*
- *For a caramel-like flavor, you can also make a version with brown sugar.*
- *Either way, top with a sprinkle of ground cinnamon.*

Every breath is a chance to restart your day.
If you're feeling overwhelmed, inhale deeply
through your nose and exhale slowly.
Now is as good a time as any!

Treat yourself to a real breakfast—the kind your mother would have made for you when you were little. And what's more soul-nourishing than pancakes? This recipe includes vanilla Greek yogurt for extra protein and flavor, and takes just five minutes to make. (Better yet, prepare the batter the night before so you're ready to go!)

- *Heat a skillet on low while you prepare the batter.*
- *In a bowl, beat two eggs. Stir in ¾ cup vanilla or plain Greek yogurt, ¼ cup of milk, 3 Tbsp. melted butter, a dash of vanilla extract, 1 cup flour, 2 tsp. baking powder, and a dash of salt and sugar. If the batter is thicker than you'd like, you can add a little extra milk at the end.*
- *Melt butter into the pan and ladle in a pancake.*
- *When you see bubbles starting to form, it's time to flip!*

Book a winter weekend at an off-season beach resort. The prices are low, you'll have the coastline to yourself—and the sound of the waves is good for the soul regardless of the water temperature.

"Success is getting what you want;

happiness is wanting what you get."

~ INGRID BERGMAN

For no-fail relaxation, lock yourself
in the bathroom and take one part privacy
and one part quiet, then add some hot water
to this homemade, soothing bath salt recipe:

- *Mix together 2 cups Epsom salts, 1 cup baking soda, and a few drops of any essential oil you like—geranium or lavender are great choices.*

Start with this thought, every morning,

even when your alarm goes off too early:

Every day is a gift.

*"Maybe happiness didn't have to be
about the big, sweeping circumstances,
about having everything in your life
in place. Maybe it was about
stringing together a bunch
of small pleasures."*

~ ANN BRASHARES
The Sisterhood of the Traveling Pants

Nothing can calm you down like a vent session
with your best friend. If that person lives far away,
schedule a drink date, pour yourselves glasses
of wine, and settle in for a long phone call
or Skype session.

Make a playlist of your favorite songs

from high school and sing along at the top

of your lungs while you remember

what it was like to have *real* problems.

Find your closest farmers market. Once a week,
bring a bag and stock up on beautiful, local foods
and interesting conversations with the people who
grew or made them. Ask for their favorite recipes
to make with your bounty! Connecting with
other people and making yourself feel cared for
are two ways to soothe the soul.

"Stop a minute, right where you are.
Relax your shoulders; shake your head
and spine like a dog shaking off cold water.
Tell that imperious voice in your head
to be still."

~ BARBARA KINGSOLVER

Acknowledgments

There is not one woman who goes it (sanely) alone.
I am so grateful for never having to fake independence
thanks to what we all have—extraordinary female friends
at the ready just waiting to help if only we learn how
to ask. Thank you for teaching me how, and for always
answering the call. In front of you I take deep breaths,
except when I am gasping for it laughing. A special thanks
to all at National Geographic who made this book happen,
and happen so . . . calmly: Hilary Black, Allyson Dickman,
Katie Olsen, Melissa Farris, and Laura Lakeway. I am also
incredibly lucky to have a devoted partner who makes me
laugh even more often than he talks me down, for which
there are never enough words of gratitude. And for all the
inspiring teachers who remind us to continue practicing
this thing called life with great humor and forgiveness,
to ourselves above all, *namaste*.

About the Author

Rebecca Ascher-Walsh is a New York–based journalist who has written for outlets including *Entertainment Weekly*, the *Los Angeles Times*, the *Wall Street Journal*, and the Huffington Post. The author of *Devoted* and founder of the Deja Foundation, which assists rescue dogs, she and her husband have a chance to practice daily calm thanks to twin daughters and their separation-anxiety-riddled but beloved rescue dog, Buddy.

Illustrations Credits

1, Bird In Paradise/Shutterstock; 2, Eric Isselee/Shutterstock; 9, Jill Ferry/Getty Images; 10, Radius Images/Corbis; 11, iStock.com/Kathy Burns-Millyard; 12-13, Jill Ferry/Trevillion Images; 14, Margaret Rowe/Getty Images; 15, PLAINVIEW/Getty Images; 16-17, iStock.com/Morgan_studio; 19, DanielW/Shutterstock; 20-21, iStock.com/konradlew; 23, iStock.com/xubingruo; 24-25, iStock.com/Morgan_studio; 27, Jill Ferry/Arcangel Images; 28-29, AFP/Getty Images; 30, Ev Thomas/Shutterstock; 31, Nattika/Shutterstock; 33, narvikk/Getty Images; 34-35, bikeriderlondon/Shutterstock; 37, project1photography/Shutterstock; 38, marilyn barbone/Shutterstock; 39, Ariwasabi/Shutterstock; 40-41, iStock.com/silatip; 43, Jill Ferry/Trevillion Images; 44-45, iStock.com/Morgan_studio; 46, Leigh Prather/Shutterstock; 47, iStock.com/CostinT; 49, iStock.com/R0b; 50-51, WorldWide/Shutterstock; 53, Jill Ferry/Getty Images; 54-55, iStock.com/anyaberkut; 57, Funny Solution Studio/Shutterstock; 58-59, iStock.com/karammiri; 60, iStock.com/gunnar3000; 61, Sabina Dimitriu/Shutterstock; 63, Subbotina Anna/Shutterstock; 64-65, Darrell Gulin/Getty Images; 67, Pavel Bobrovskiy/Shutterstock; 68-69, Detchart Sukchit/Shutterstock; 70, iStock.com/tedestudio; 71, Elnur/Shutterstock; 72-73, iStock.com/lubb; 75, Marysckin/Shutterstock; 76-77, iStock.com/mattjeacock; 79, Grace Chon/Getty Images; 80-81, iStock.com/STILLFX; 82, monticello/Shutterstock; 83, iStock.com/malerapaso; 85, Georgianna Lane/Garden Photo World/Corbis; 86-87, iStock.com/IakovKalinin; 89, Tim Fitzharris/Minden Pictures/Corbis; 90, gururugu/

READ. BREATHE. RELAX.
with *National Geographic Books*

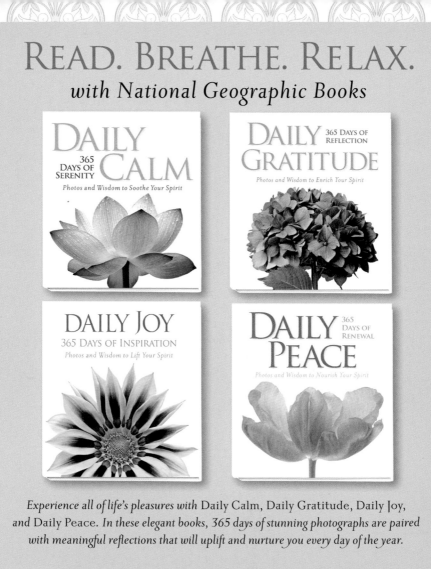

Experience all of life's pleasures with Daily Calm, Daily Gratitude, Daily Joy, and Daily Peace. In these elegant books, 365 days of stunning photographs are paired with meaningful reflections that will uplift and nurture you every day of the year.

AVAILABLE WHEREVER BOOKS ARE SOLD
nationalgeographic.com/books